Ben Wicks'
How To Draw

Cartoons

PROSPERO
B·O·O·K·S
A DIVISION OF CHAPTERS INC.

Created by Ben Wicks for
Prospero Books, a division of Chapters Inc.

Published in 1998 by
Ben Wicks and Associates
449A Jarvis Street
Toronto, Ontario
M4Y 2G8

Includes index.
ISBN 1-895651-22-0

Printed & bound in Canada.

TABLE OF CONTENTS

LET'S GET STARTED

INTRODUCTION

Although I have had more than twenty jobs since I left school at 14 years of age, none, not even being a professional musician, has given me more pleasure than that of being a professional cartoonist.

I began at an early age. Finding school a miserable experience, I spent my days scribbling in school books and waiting for the art class to begin.

Fortunately, the art teacher, who was also the math teacher, knew nothing about art and, rather than criticize my work, was quite happy to see me scribble away and enjoy myself.

So it was that I learned an early lesson - one that I never forgot.

Anyone can cartoon. Even I can, someone who was hopeless at most things.

The fact is, cartooning is extremely easy to do.

Although I am a professional cartoonist who has drawn for leading newspapers and magazines around the world, don't feel that I am any better or worse at drawing than you.

INTRODUCTION

Let's face it. This is not going to be a contest.
We're not about to enter an Olympic race,
or knock over a Sumo wrestler.

We are going to enjoy ourselves.

So sit back and relax. This is just the
beginning. We're about to drift through
these pages and cartoon all manner of things.

Although I cannot guarantee that you will be as
successful as Walt Disney or the Doonsbury or Dilbert cartoonists,
I can absolutely promise you one thing. You're going to learn to do
something that will give you pleasure for the rest of your life.

1 WHAT DO WE NEED?

Naturally, as with most things, we're going to need some tools before we start.

The good news is that the tools we do need are few and uncomplicated. We are not about to build a house or perform brain surgery.

Even the cost of our equipment is something we can all afford. In fact, what we need to start on our merry way can be measured in coins.

So what do we need?

Something that is already easy to find around the house. Reach out your hand.

Now take that silly piece of wood with the lead sticking out of one end and put the black piece against a sheet of paper. Now move it around the surface.

That, my friend, is a cartoon. Okay, so it's not a face. Give us a little time and it will soon become a Mona Lisa or anything else that we will be proud to show to our friends.

WHAT DO WE NEED?

But not yet.

For now I want to concentrate on the pencil.

Most artists will tell you that there are a whole range of different pencils.

There are.

But at the risk of getting too classy at this stage, we're going to concentrate on the few that will give you the best results.

Since we're at the beginning of our cartooning, we are sure to make lines on the paper that we're not happy with.

MOM

NOT GOOD

DAD

WORSE

For this reason, we need a pencil that's makes a mark that's easy to get rid of.

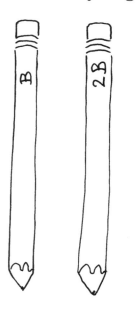

At the end of most pencils, you'll find a mark that lets you know the kind of pencil it is. The mark is a method of grading the pencils. What we're looking for is a couple of pencils marked 'B' or '2B'.

The beauty of these pencils is that the lines they make can easily be erased without leaving a mark on the paper. There are other pencils with softer grades, however, you will find that the marks you make with these will no doubt smudge.

WHAT DO WE NEED?

No one wants to be constantly rubbing out smudges on the paper or washing his or her hands to get rid of the smudge marks after every drawing. So, when we think of pencils, it's the old 'B' or '2B' for us.

You'll need an eraser. Avoid the harder eraser. They can easily destroy the surfaces of most drawing paper, leaving behind ugly marks.

I use a soft eraser. Although these soft ones leave behind tiny pieces of eraser across the drawing, they can easily be brushed aside, leaving the surface of the paper still in fine shape for drawing once again.

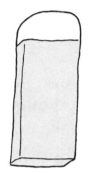

Naturally, you'll need to keep the pencil sharpened.

I once had an art teacher who insisted that the only way to sharpen a pencil was to use a sharp knife.

After most of the class lost a couple of fingers, we quickly lost interest in this method of sharpening pencils and reverted to the best way of all, the pencil sharpener.

These come in all shapes and sizes. Some screw to tables and have a handle attached, while others work on a battery and, the moment the pencil is shoved in its opening, a fine point suddenly appears.

For us, we need nothing so fancy. I have a small metal pencil sharpener in my drawer and when I need a point on my pencil, out it comes. I believe it cost me 20 cents ten years ago. Today, however, it could be as much as 25 cents.

WHAT DO WE NEED?

The point I'm trying to make is this. We are at an early stage in learning how to draw cartoons.

We are not preparing for a showing of our work at an art gallery or selling our work at an auction.

As we progress, we will find ourselves wanting to make sure our cartoons stay on the paper long enough for us to frame them.

Most professional cartoonists feel the same way and, since they are anxious to see their work reproduced in the various newspapers and magazines, they know that they will need to make a line stronger than that made by a pencil.

What we're going to need now is a pen.

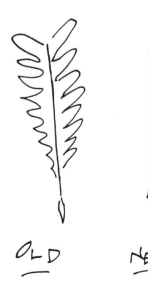

Although we're at the beginning stages, there is no time like the present to get comfortable using a pen.

Who knows? Your first cartoon may be a masterpiece so we certainly need to make that one permanent for posterity.

But what about the mess? Never fear. We are well beyond the quill and feather days.

WHAT DO WE NEED?

Using a pen today is a piece of cake. No longer do cartoonists find themselves dipping a pen in an ink well and dripping most of it down the front of a clean shirt.

We don't have to worry about a favourite nib or cleaning the pen after use. Today, we have a whole wealth of pens that require nothing more than removing the cap before grabbing our pad and starting to draw.

So let's get down to your local art store to see what they have on the pen rack. You'll be amazed. There are pens of all shapes and sizes.

Some make a thin line. Some make a fat line. Some make a line that's not so fat as a fat line and others make a line that's not as thin as a thin line. Just take one and try it out on the scribble pad that's usually right beside the display.

WHAT DO WE NEED?

Make sure that the pen is waterproof. In this way, we can guarantee that it won't smudge if our hand rests on the line.

Keep away from technical pens or pens for professional designers and architects. They know how to use them. I don't and, quite frankly, I don't wish to. We are going to cartoon and have fun. Not design a second Taj Mahal.

Just one other point. Although you will find pens that draw in most colours, stick to black.

Some reading this will be anxious to grab a brush and start sloshing around the paper. I never ever use a brush. Some cartoonists do, but I don't.

I find that there are plenty of felt pens that will fill in most of the areas that should be black.

As for using a roller. Forget it!

WHAT DO WE NEED?

Paper.

There's lots of it around. All types. Shiny, smooth, rough and textured. Light-weight and heavy. Coloured. White and grey.

Let's keep it simple - the cheap stuff. A good pad of inexpensive photocopying paper is all we need to start.

If we mess up our picture, who cares? We just tear out the page and start again (don't forget to recycle!).

Just make sure that the paper has a fairly smooth surface and that the pad is not too big. It should be just comfortable enough to rest on your lap, especially if you plan to draw outside.

Before you leave the art shop, have a look at a pad that's small enough to slip in your pocket. Pay for it first!

It can be fun to whip it out when on a train or bus and have a crack at drawing your fellow passengers.

WHAT DO WE NEED?

The more you draw, the better you will become.

Up until now, we have dealt with the material we need before we start cartooning.

Don't forget.

- **Pencils** - preferably 'B' or '2B'.

- A nice soft **eraser**. One that is too hard will damage the paper.

- A small pocket **pencil sharpener**.

- Get down to your local art shop and find some **pens**. It doesn't have to be ink. We're not in the middle ages.

- Keep it **black**. I myself use a Pilot drawing pen, however, there are many to choose from.

- A nice pad of cheap **paper** should round off the shopping list. And don't forget the smooth surface in a pad that's comfortable.

That's it!

Fasten your seat belt. We're about to take off for the world of cartooning.

2 WHEN TO CARTOON

"Where is the best place?" Wherever you are most comfortable.

"You mean sitting in front of the T.V.?" Why not?

There's lots to draw and, since most of the people on the screen are moving around, this will force you to draw pretty fast. In this way, you will begin to relax more and scribble the lines that you are making, giving each line more action. But I'm getting ahead of myself. We'll cover these areas later in the book.

Where is the best place to draw cartoons?

When I lived in Calgary, a Western town in the centre of Canada, I began to draw. We were living in one room, with a small kitchen and a bed that came out of the wall.

WHEN TO CARTOON

Being a milkman (one of many jobs), I was home early with little to do but wait for my wife, who was a nurse, to arrive home.

I decided on a hobby and bought a book, similar to this one (though not as good), on cartooning.

I did as instructed and began sending my work to various magazines.

For fun, I started with the world's leading magazine, the *Saturday Evening Post*. Six weeks later, they wrote to say they would buy the work. I drew for them for three years.

So where is the best place to work?

Anywhere you have available. I draw in my office in Toronto on an old office desk. No easel or expensive drawing table. Just a regular flat surface with room for my paper, pen and pencil.

For you, a space in the house where you are comfortable, with a good light, will make it that much easier to draw.

Try to keep the same spot, too. It does make it easier to store your materials and drawings that you wish to keep.

Certainly, if there are little ones around the house, your drawings will need to be in a safe spot.

WHEN TO CARTOON

Now to the question of when you should draw...

I, myself, prefer the morning. It's the time I have set aside for more than thirty years.

The ideas seem to come a lot faster before 12 noon.

There are times when deadlines have forced me to think of ideas in the afternoon. I always find it more difficult.

Since we are at the beginning stage, any time you decide to put pencil to paper is a good time. You may enjoy getting up early in the morning. The house is quiet and there's no one around to look over your shoulder as you draw.

WHEN TO CARTOON

Quite possibly, at first, you may feel that your drawings are not ready to show. Most of us felt the same way.

The wonderful thing is that cartooning is so easy to do that, within weeks, you'll be so excited that you'll be showing your drawings to friends and family and asking them what they think.

Trust me. By the end of this book, I'll have competition.

Remember.

• The best place to draw in the house is where you are most **comfortable**.

• Make sure you have **decent light**. Drawing in the dark can produce terrible results.

• Drawing in **front of the T.V.** can give you plenty of subjects to draw.

• Keep the **same place** in the house or apartment. It's much easier to store your material and save your work. You'll definitely want to keep track of your drawings.

• Try drawing in a pad. It makes it possible to follow your progress. I still have the first cartoon that was bought by the *Saturday Evening Post*. It's actually a good reminder of how badly I drew when I started and how much I've improved since then.

3 TIME TO DRAW

Let's begin by understanding what we're going to learn as we turn the pages of this book. This is not a 'how-to' book on becoming a famous artist. What we are going to do is draw pictures that are funny, cartoon characters that attract the reader's attention. Famous cartoon characters that we see on television today do just that. They are, first and foremost, funny to look at.

So where should we start? The answer is easy - at the top, of course.

The Head.

Okay. Draw a simple orange-shaped circle. Before you do touch the paper, just hold the pencil and draw circles in the air. Now continue the circular motion and touch the paper. It's a wonderful way to loosen up.

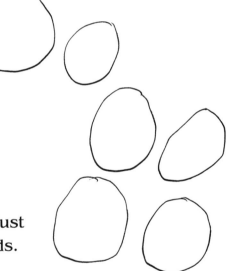

Draw orange shaped circles of all sizes and, just for fun, try drawing the circles with both hands.

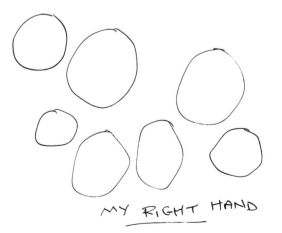

MY RIGHT HAND

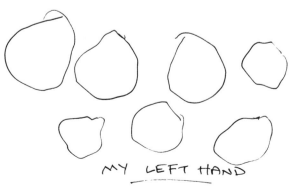

MY LEFT HAND

TIME TO DRAW

Don't worry about drawing a perfect circle. Since no one I know can draw an exact circle, there's no reason you should worry about it. Indeed, the shape we are going to need is more like an orange.

So, let's have a look at what you've done.

What you should have is a series of interesting shapes that have begun to take on the appearance of a drawing that is somewhat funny to look at.

Okay, so the shapes are not all that great. Who do you know that has a perfectly orange-shaped head?

The Face.

It tells all. Is the person sad? Is the person happy? Is the person angry? Is the person surprised or contented?

We're going to soon find out. Just grab your pad of paper with the orange-shaped circles and we'll find out how your cartoon head feels.

A Start by drawing a faint line down the centre of our orange, from top to bottom. This will give us a guide to the middle of the face.

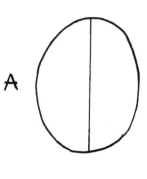

B Now draw a faint line across, a little less than half way down.

We now have some idea where to place the eyes.

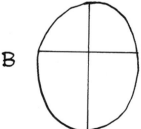

TIME TO DRAW

C Look in the mirror. See how the eyes are lined up with the top of the nose?

Now we know where the nose begins.

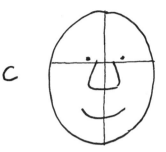

D Draw the nose and then the ears from the side of the head and we have our first cartoon face.

We've looked at cartooning the face from the front. It's time to draw the head from different angles.

Three-Quarter Angle.

It's not as easy as head-on but it can be made easier by first drawing your orange shape for the head.

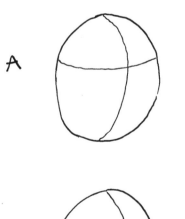

A Draw a guide line from top to bottom, as I have done here. All we need is a line across and we'll be ready to begin.

B Let's start with the nose. Position it to start coming out of the head at the crossing point where both lines meet.

Now bring the underline of the nose base to the top-to-bottom line.

So far, so good.

TIME TO DRAW

C To be able to really see that this is a head, we will need the eyes. I've positioned mine on either side of the nose, this time along the line that runs across. Notice how the eyes are pretty much the same distance apart from the crossing point.

C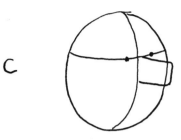

D At this point, what's needed is a mouth to show expression. Add an ear and some hair and our first cartoon head from a three-quarter angle is complete.

D

Side View.

I find this the easiest of all angles when drawing a head. It's known as the profile and consists of the head, an eye, the nose, an ear and the mouth.

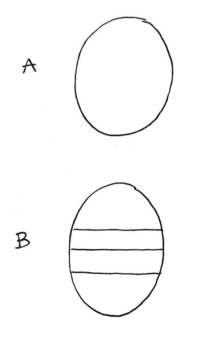

A Let's start with our old favourite, the orange.

B Just a few faint guide lines running across the head and we're ready to place our nose, eye, mouth and ear.

TIME TO DRAW

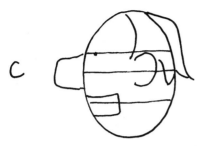

C Draw your nose above and below the centre line.

Now place the eye in line with the top of the nose.

The top of the ear begins at the top line.

The mouth is placed on the bottom line.

Now add hair.

D Remove guide lines and meet your new cartoon character.

Head Shapes.

Not all heads are shaped the same. Just look around you. Some are square. Some are long. Others are round and still others are pear-shaped.

The square
Tough
and rugged.

Pear-shaped
Could do with
a good work out.

Round
Jolly and
full of fun.

TIME TO DRAW

Try making your own faces out of these three shapes.

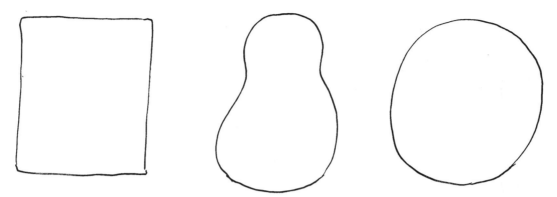

Let's pick up our pencils and start tackling some of the shapes that make up the human race.

The shape and size of the head are usually clues to the rest of a person's body.

TIME TO DRAW

Here are some of mine. I'm sure you can do better.

There are dozens of different head shapes and, as we progress, you'll notice the one that fits the kind of person you have drawn in your cartoon.

It's time to move on.

What we have at the moment are dozens of shapes with a nose, eyes, ears and a mouth attached. We have no idea how these heads feel.

We're about to find out. Our faces are about to express feelings. So, once again, let's get drawing those orange shapes and find out how our cartoon heads are feeling.

4 EXPRESSIONS

Let's go back to the mirror. It's the perfect place to find a cheap model. Twist your face into different shapes. Let's begin by dreaming that you have an A plus on your exam or have just won the lottery. How do you feel? Now what do you see in the mirror?

Draw our orange shape once more.

Fill in the space by looking in the mirror and copying what you see. Since we're feeling good about ourselves, we're going to begin with a smile. No teeth showing, just a nice big grin.

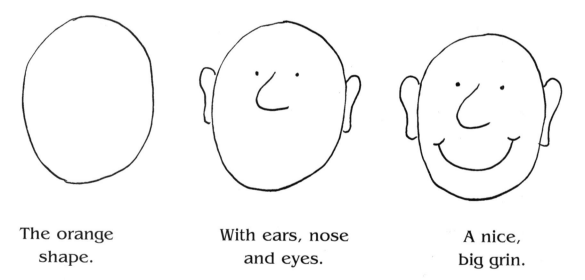

| The orange shape. | With ears, nose and eyes. | A nice, big grin. |

Look in the mirror. Notice that when we smile with our mouths closed, we puff out our cheeks. To show this effect, all we need is a couple of tiny lines on each end of our mouth line.

So we're in a good mood, are we? Then let's see how we feel if we're even happier.

EXPRESSIONS

It's time to draw the face of someone who is truly happy. When we smile, our mouth turns up at the sides. When we laugh, our mouth opens wide.

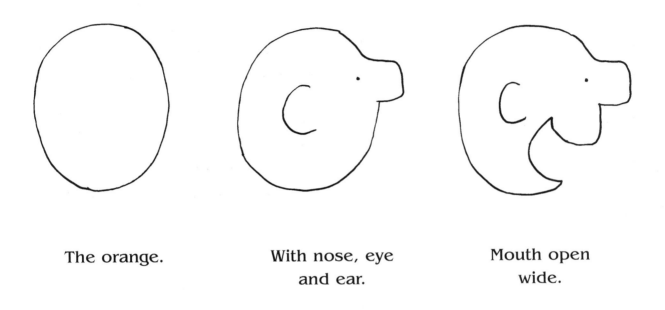

The orange.

With nose, eye and ear.

Mouth open wide.

You're Sad. Just take the line that you drew for a smile and turn it down on the ends.

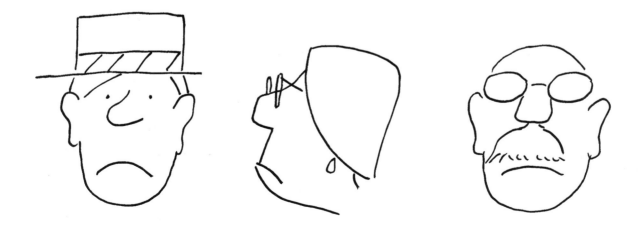

EXPRESSIONS

You're Angry. It's simple to do. Just turn the mouth line into your sad look. Now draw your eyebrows sloping down until they are almost touching the eyes.

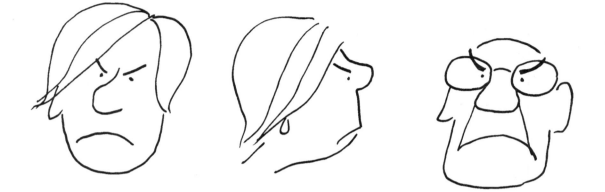

You're Terrified. Whatever it is that you've seen, you wished it were somewhere else. Maybe it's a ghost or maybe it's a space monster. How do you feel you'd react?

Now look in the mirror and see what has happened to your face. Your mouth has dropped open. You want to scream but you can't. If you have hair, it is now standing on end. Your eyebrows have lifted almost off the top of your head.

Now that's scared.

EXPRESSIONS

You're Surprised. It's your birthday and, without your knowing, all of your friends have thrown you a surprise party.

Just lift the eyebrows from the middle and open the mouth.

You're Really Surprised. The Spice Girls have shown up.

It was a great party and now everyone feels that it's time to go home. How do we know? Because they're beginning to feel sleepy.

EXPRESSIONS

The Sleepy Look. Just close the eyes, open the mouth a little and your drawing is ready for bed.

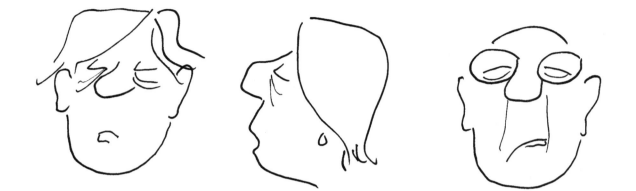

Another reminder.

*   Go to the mirror and **make faces**.

*   Draw the orange shape and add nose, eyes, ears and mouth.

*   For the **smile** just lift the corners of the mouth.

*   For the **sad** look just turn the same corners down.

*   Your **angry.** The mouth turns down and the eyebrows turn down and almost touch the eyes.

*   You're **terrified**. Lift the eyebrows and open the mouth.

*   You're **surprised**. Lift the eyebrows, open the mouth and laugh.

*   **Sleepy?** Just close the eyes and open the mouth a little.

5 LET'S DRAW PEOPLE

Look at the most important thing about drawing people - how to cartoon a man and how to cartoon a woman.

This most obvious difference is usually the hair. Not always, but for the sake of our drawing, women usually have longer hair. Let's give it a try.

Where's our old favourite, the orange shape?

You see?

Your orange is getting better with every try. Now, let's give it some hair.

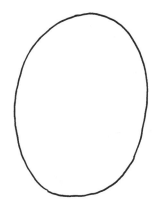

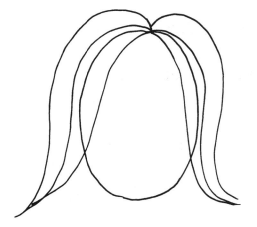

What have we got?

We've got an orange with hair - not the kind of attractive female we had in mind.

Although very attractive to another orange, it doesn't do much for us.

But it's a start.

LET'S DRAW PEOPLE

Now, let's add a cute little nose, a full mouth and eyes to finish her face off.

Now for cartooning men. It's simple. Once again we take our orange shape and, by following a few simple rules, we will find ourselves drawing a man. Many men lose their hair as they get older. On the top of their head, that is. Some have beards and still others have a moustache. Santa has both a beard and a moustache.

I'm going to let you try your hand at drawing men. Here are some of mine. All of these began with the orange shape.

LET'S DRAW PEOPLE

If you feel at a loss for faces, just look around you or, better yet, have a look at some magazines. You'll find lots of men and women, some happy, some sad, but all looking different.

The fact is that not everyone looks the same. Fortunately, we live in a world that is full of people whose colour and appearance is different. What a boring world this would be if we were all the same. No one would know who was whom. So before we move on, let's do a variety of drawings showing men and women of different colour and cultural background.

Notice that in depicting a darker skin I have drawn a series of lines across the face. It's a simple method of shading when using a pen or pencil but certainly not the only way, as those with a computer will no doubt know.

LET'S DRAW PEOPLE

Drawing the orange shape for the head has been fun, it's true, but we're not going to be happy with a lot of oranges running around the house. We all know that there is more to the human being than the head.

Get ready to tackle the rest of the human form. The easiest way to draw a figure has been famous since the days of the cave man. It's known as the **stick figure**, or as some call it, the **match-stick figure**. It is so simple to draw that I'm sure you'll have no difficulty.

A Begin with your orange shape.

B Now draw a straight line from the bottom of the orange.

C Now two short lines across from which our arms and legs will hang.

D All we need to complete our matchstick figure is a couple of circles at the bottom of the legs and arms for the feet and hands.

This figure may look like it hasn't had a meal for years. Yet it is the basis of our cartoon figure.

Alright. Take this figure and get it moving across the paper. Ready? Then let's go.

LET'S DRAW PEOPLE

Let's draw our match-stick figure in different positions. Think of the figure as someone really energetic. It has been standing on the paper doing nothing. It's time for it to move around.

Here are some 'action' match-sticks. Have a look at them and try some for yourself. Is someone in the house sitting in a chair? Try them as a match-stick figure. You'll soon get the hang of the exercise and have lots of fun as you do so.

LET'S DRAW PEOPLE

People come in all shapes and sizes. Some are tall, some are short, some are fat and some are thin. Try to fill out your match-stick drawings and show them for the true figures they really are.

Take a close look at the people who live in your house. How do they differ? Certainly, your friends do not all look the same.

What do they really look like?

Is one tall and one short?

LET'S DRAW PEOPLE

Is one young and one very old?

Although each of these drawings started out as match-figures, I want you to now start drawing by using a rough outline. We know that we can easily scribble our orange for the head. So why not continue to scribble?

Just take a pencil and scribble. Try to use the whole arm to draw. Don't make each line perfect. All this will do is give you a very static drawing. Although what we are doing is drawing cartoons, this is an art form and we are producing a picture.

Let's take a few minutes and go to town. Scribble. That's it, all over the pad.

Keep scribbling and draw a head.

Without taking the pencil off the paper, start drawing a body.

Now hold up your picture. Isn't it a wonderful mess? Of course it is and it's also a much more interesting picture than one that was drawn slowly with your head practically touching the paper.

LET'S DRAW PEOPLE

You're not convinced? Okay, stand aside. Here comes my pencil to scribble a series of figures.

The series of drawings you have just made have action written all over them. The lines do move, however, let's get back to drawing the cartoon figure and a major area that we have yet to cover.

Without knowing how to draw these areas of the human figure, our characters would have difficulty picking up a pencil and would really find it an effort to walk.

Do you know what it is that we've missed? Right. It's hands and feet.

6 HANDS AND FEET

I can remember that when I began drawing cartoons for magazines, the most difficult thing I found was to draw hands and feet.

I was so nervous about being seen that I had this difficulty that I choose to draw most of my figures behind a desk with their hands in their pockets in order to hide this fact.

There is no doubt that, in the world of art, hands are the most difficult to draw well.

Leonardo Da Vinci may have had no problem painting hands, however, most of us do. I mention this at the start to offset any feeling you may have that your hands are so bad, the only answer is to burn this book.

Don't do that. Despite the fact that the hands we're about to draw would have Da Vinci rolling around the floor with laughter, we are going to learn to draw hands that are not only passable, they would give most cartoonists a great sense of accomplishment.

HANDS AND FEET

Let me begin by giving you a short cut.

To draw hands in a cartoon, you have to place them in the right spot - on the ends of arms.

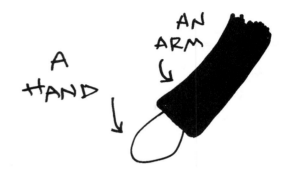

Obviously, this blob of whatever seen on the right must be a hand. It certainly isn't a foot. Undoubtedly, the placing of a hand is the vital first step.

This is okay provided the hand is on the end of an arm. What if we need the hand to do something? What if it were holding a can of pop or a baseball bat or a pair of ballet shoes? Now we must get down to the real business of drawing a hand.

"Oh, no." I can hear you say. "I've tried this before and try as I may I can't draw hands." I'm sorry to disagree. Yes, you can. Your problem is that you are trying too hard to draw something that is extremely difficult to draw.

Forget about drawing a hand. Let's try something that's much more simple and looks like a hand.

Hold a hand up in front of you. What does it look like? I know it looks like a hand but what else?

It looks like a bunch of bananas, right?

HANDS AND FEET

If you were asked to draw a bunch of bananas, what would it look like? Hopefully, it would look like what I've drawn.

But is this a hand? You're right. It's not. It's still a bunch of bananas that looks like a hand. We're on our way, though. We've made a start. We can now draw something that looks like a hand.

It's time to move on and where better than to go back to our old friend, the match stick figure?

A Draw the top of the figure with the arms coming out and place circles for hands on the end of the arms.

B Now draw small lines, representing fingers, from the hands. This is the hand most cartoonists draw.

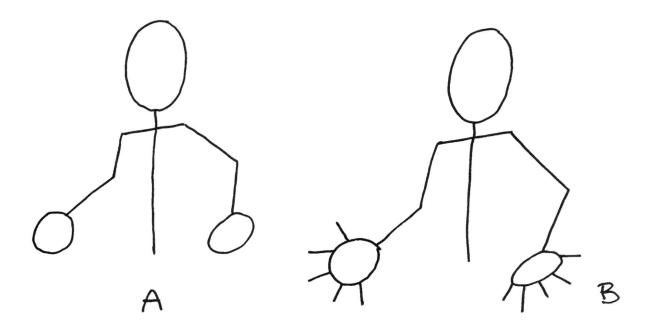

Now, let's take a close up and add to our drawing of the hand.

HANDS AND FEET

A First draw our
orange shape.

B Now draw five lines
coming from it.

C Fatten them up as
though they
were sausages.

D Take away the
guide lines. Add a
small line to show
the palm and what
have you got?

A nice hand.

Don't worry about
fingernails.
Remember.
We are drawing
a cartoon figure.

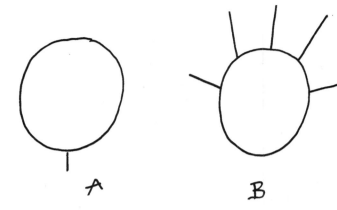

In fact, many cartoonists continue to do what Disney did when he first
drew Mickey Mouse. They draw just three fingers and a thumb on a
hand. If Walt Disney wasn't worried about the accurate drawing of a
hand, why should we?

We're almost ready to begin drawing our hands in a series of action
poses. Before you do, take another look at your hand. Bend the thumb
and fingers very slightly. Notice the little curved line that appears at the
bottom of the fingers and where the thumb joins the palm of the hand.

HANDS AND FEET

We can easily copy this by drawing the curve lines of our own. Here are just three examples of what you might see when you take this look at your hand.

By now we should feel better about drawing a hand, so let's get the hand working for us. As you know, our hands are used in all manner of ways. We can use them as a means of expressing ourselves :

- Show a person the direction they should go.
- Show that you feel okay.
- Ask for change.
- Offer a can of pop.
- Did you like the performance?

You've got the idea.

Now see how many hands you can draw that are telling something.

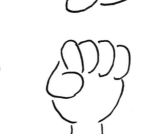

HANDS AND FEET

How to attach the hand to the arm.

Once we place our hands on the ends of arms, they can tell us all manner of things by their action.

I surrender.   Give me a hug.   Vote for me.

One more important thing to remember when drawing fingers for your figures is to make sure the thumb is on the correct side of the hand.

Just stand upright with your arms to your side. Notice how the thumbs are to the front.

All too often, I have finished a drawing and found that I have made the simple mistake of placing the thumb on the wrong side of the hand. By far, the best method of checking your drawing when you finish is to hold the drawing up in front of a mirror. It's amazing how quickly you will spot a mistake.

HANDS AND FEET

Now to the feet.

Once again it's a matter of placement.
If what you draw are on the end of
legs, there's a very good chance that
they will turn out to be feet.

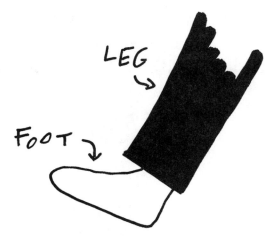

As with hands, feet are not the
easiest to draw.

Why?

To find the answer, we need to start by removing a shoe. If you're
wearing a shoe, that is. Now remove your sock or stocking and take a
look at what it is that's staring back at you.

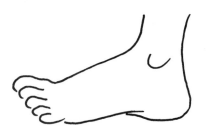

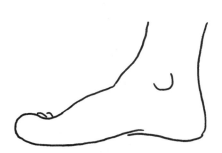

It's not the prettiest part of the body. Just don't worry too much if your
drawing of feet turns out to be pretty ugly.

HANDS AND FEET

The main thing we're looking for in a foot is balance. The foot is the object that gives the rest of the body balance. Draw feet the wrong way and the body will begin to fall over.

Once you understand this fact, the rest is pretty easy.

So let's get cracking and have a go at drawing a foot. One advantage that we have is to be able to look at our own feet when drawing them.

Taking one foot at a time, you'll notice that most of us have five toes and a heel.

Note that the big toe is the one that's on the inside of the foot and that it points up when the others point down.

HANDS AND FEET

Naturally, the simplest feet to draw are those that are wearing some form of shoe. Let's start with the house slipper. It has no heel and comfortably covers the foot. Without toes to worry about, it's the easiest to draw.

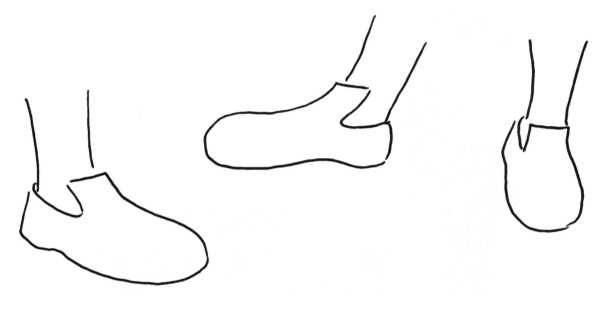

Now for men's shoes.

HANDS AND FEET

What about the difficult women's high heeled shoes?

Running shoes.

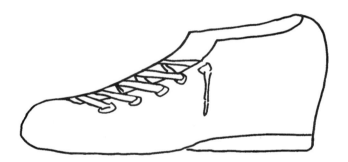

Yet the only problem with the shoes that we've drawn is that most cartoonists would never draw shoes to look like this. Why? Because they are not a cartoonist's shoe.

Most, including myself, are quite content to give the appearance of a shoe and feel that if it's on the end of a leg and covering a foot it must be a shoe.

So if you find drawing shoes difficult, don't worry. Over time, you'll develop your own style.

HANDS AND FEET

Just grab the newspaper and have a look at some of the feet drawn by professional cartoonists. You'll be surprised how unlike feet they really are. Here are a few to make you feel better.

Ready to get the feet working? How are they when involved in sports or maybe at work? Let's try a few and don't worry too much what they look like. Just know that the role of the foot is to keep the body from falling over.

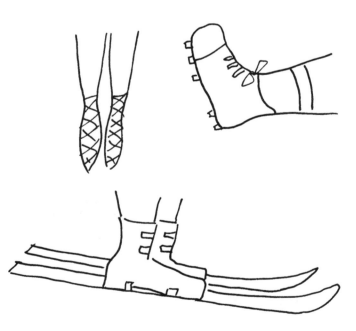

So stand back, we're about to get those feet moving. Grab your pencil and, whatever it is you love to do, get those feet involved.

HANDS AND FEET

Don't forget.

- Hands and feet are difficult to draw.

- Place them in the right spot, with hands on the end of arms and feet on the end of legs.

- At first, try drawing a bunch of bananas for hands.

- Then draw the match-stick figure. Draw circles on the end of the lines for arms.

- Draw five lines from there to show placement of finger and thumb.

- Now fatten them up.

- Remember to place the thumb on the correct side of the hand.

- Check by holding your drawing in front of a mirror.

- As with hands, it's a matter of placement. Feet go on the end of legs.

- Feet help to balance the body.

- The big toe is on the inside of the foot.

- When drawing footwear, start with a slipper.

- Stop worrying about what the feet you've drawn look like.

- Look at the comics to see how other cartoonists draw feet.

- Didn't I tell you that your feet and hands are as good as theirs?

7 LET'S GET DRESSED

The wonderful thing about dressing cartoon figures is the amount of models we have available. We live in a visual world. Everywhere we look there are pictures of people dressed in all sorts of clothing.

For our purposes, though, let's deal with the ones closest to home. By now, we have a good idea of how to draw something that looks like a figure. All we need to do is throw some clothes on it.

Before we do, here's a simple approach. Since the figures are the difficult thing to draw, let's put them to one side and start with the object at hand, the clothes.

They're easy to draw and, once we've finished them, we can easily fit the body into the clothes. Let's begin with men and one of the easiest and most common articles of clothing.

The t-shirt.

LET'S GET DRESSED

Add some trousers and a few finishing touches, and we have a man dressed in a t-shirt and trousers.

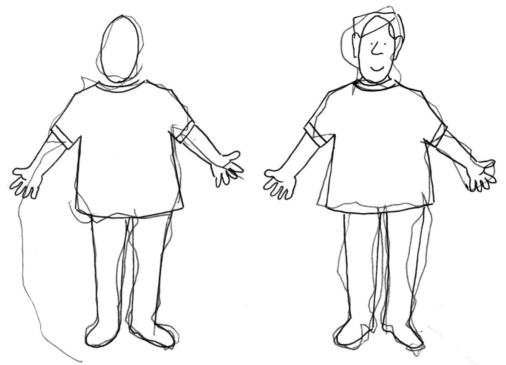

Try dressing a woman. It's just as easy as dressing a man. Draw a dress and place a woman inside. Add those little touches, like hair, face and shoes, and our figure is finished.

LET'S GET DRESSED

Now we're really cooking. Drawing clothes and placing figures inside is working so let's wrap this up with one more figure, a young boy.

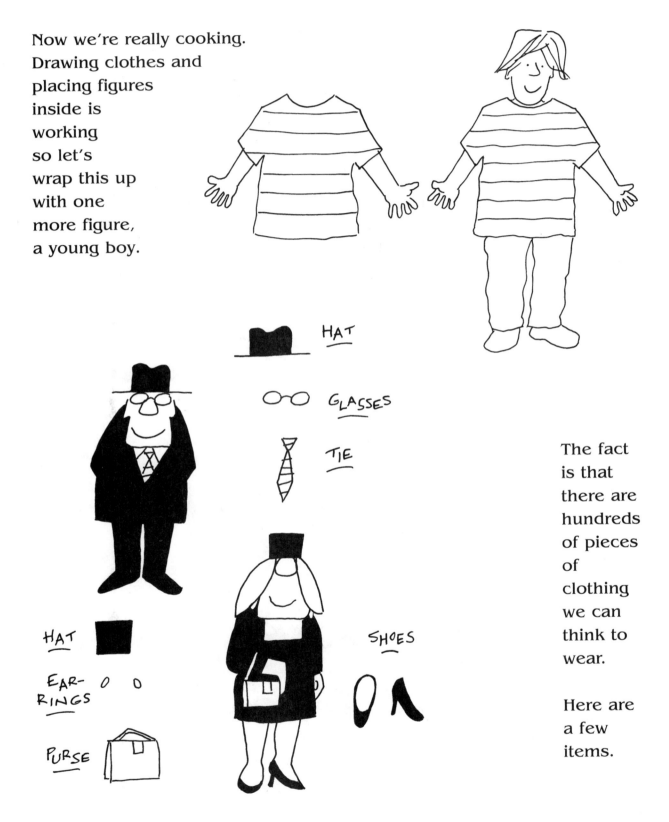

HAT

GLASSES

TIE

HAT

EAR-RINGS o o

PURSE

SHOES

The fact is that there are hundreds of pieces of clothing we can think to wear.

Here are a few items.

LET'S GET DRESSED

Try drawing them alone, then add your figure.

HAT

GLASSES

SCARF

FLAT
SHOES

BOW
TIE

JACKET

SHOES

8 FIGURES IN ACTION

We now have a nice little set of pieces to fit into our drawings. Unfortunately, as wonderful as they are to look at, they are pretty boring just hanging about the page.

What we need to do is make our drawings move around. If you wish, you can go back to our friend, the stick figure.

The wonderful thing about the stick figure is that there are so few lines to worry about. Getting these lines to move as a human figure, is just a matter of looking in a mirror. Whatever the pose you want to take, draw the lines of your stick figure. Here's how to make it simple. Face the mirror and draw your stick figure in the action pose you have taken.

FIGURES IN ACTION

If you decide that you want your figure to have a long, wobbly neck or short, stiff arms, it's easy to do. Just exaggerate any part of the stick figure.

Who knows? You may wish to draw a stick space creature. Maybe it's got five arms and three legs. Just add them to the orange that you've drawn for a body.

Let's get back to earth and see how our human figure is doing.

FIGURES IN ACTION

Although we have drawn our human in various positions, it's time to get dressed. Here are a few drawings of the stick figures with clothes being added.

If you need more action pictures, get a copy of a sports magazine. There's plenty of good movement in one to get your pencil flying.

FIGURES IN ACTION

Figures are all around us just waiting to be drawn. This is not a test, so don't worry about being too accurate. Just get the figure down on the page. Most people are anxious to move, so you'll need to draw fast to get the feeling of action - none of that slow, stiff drawing stuff for us. We're quick on the draw and you'd better believe it.

Don't forget that not everyone wears shirts, ties and dresses. Many people we see are in a uniform.

The real secret of being a good cartoonist is seeing more than most people do when they look around them.

FIGURES IN ACTION

Here are a few of my uniforms that I can see if I look out of the window.

I'm sure if you look around, you'll find that many people are wearing uniforms of some sort or another. Grab the pad and get them down on paper.

When we get to the section of the book dealing with funny cartoons, we will find lots of them appearing as the main character.

FIGURES IN ACTION

Remember.

- Try drawing clothes then place the figure in them.

- Start with something easy like a t-shirt.

- Move on to dressing women and youth.

- Have a crack at drawing individual pieces of clothing.

- Move your figures around by placing them in various positions.

- Grab your pad and draw the people you see around you.

- Remember that drawing is seeing. Look around you and observe.

9 SETTING THE STAGE

We have now solved the secret of how to draw the cartoon figure and, the more we draw them, the better they will become. Yet it doesn't matter how happy we are with the figure we cartoon, that figure will become pretty boring to look at unless we place it in a setting.

Most of us know this as 'background' or, as it's known in the world of the theatre, 'props'.

Certainly, if I draw a figure like this, the picture itself will not be complete unless we give some idea of where the figure is walking.

This is pretty easy to do and can be great fun.

Let's start by drawing a walking figure.

Where do you want this figure to go?

It's up to you.

No passport is needed - just your pencil and pad, and your walking friend can travel wherever you want him to go.

Think of a number of different backgrounds.

SETTING THE STAGE

Down the street.

Across a desert.

In a jungle.

Let's keep our figure outside in the fresh air and see what a few simple lines can do to show exactly where the figure is located.

In the city.

In the country.

SETTING THE STAGE

Before we end our outside section, there is one important point I wish to make. Many of the cartoon figures that we draw will be in an overseas location. Many of these cities and towns are different than the ones we call home. There is no point in placing a cartoon figure in a Middle East location that carries the same billboards and signs as at home.

How are we to know where it is that our cartoon is walking? For this reason, cartoonists draw locations that will be instantly recognized by the reader. If it's Paris, the Eiffel Tower could be in the background.

Here are a couple of examples.

A An actual middle eastern location.

B This is the one drawn for the reader of the cartoon. Remember that locations in cartoons are what the reader expect them to look like, not what they really are.

A   B

SETTING THE STAGE

Let's go inside.

This can be a little more tricky. Our figure is going to be sitting in a chair or eating at a table. The main thing to remember is that this is a cartoon and is intended to be funny, so don't fill the cartoon with furniture.

If you make your drawings too busy, the person looking at the cartoon will be so overwhelmed with the furniture that they will find it difficult to concentrate on the joke. Remember what we did with our walking figure outside - a few simple lines to suggest where he was walking?

The same goes for the inside. Before you draw furniture around the house, let's just draw a few pieces to get the hang of how simple they can be.

SETTING THE STAGE

Another good area to practice drawing is the bedroom. Imagine if you were going to build a bed. First you would need the two end pieces.

A One would be for the head of the bed and the other for the foot.

B Add a couple of lines to join these two pieces and you have a bed.

C Add a pillow.

D Then add some bed clothes and a line behind the pillow to give the drawing some depth and there you have a very nice simple cartoon bed. It's nothing fancy, just something to sleep on.

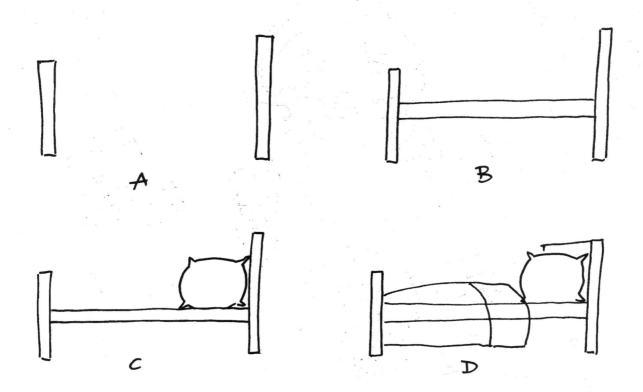

Try a few beds then start looking around the house. Just remember to keep it simple.

SETTING THE STAGE

Just think of the many items you see as boxes with legs.

Windows are just square shapes. Add some curtains, and things around your house soon get really cozy.

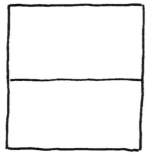 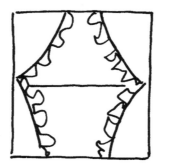 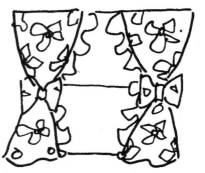

How about some photos and knickknacks to brighten up the room?

SETTING THE STAGE

Just remember not to overload your drawing.

Somewhere in the picture you're going to need a joke.

Remember.

- Fit in various backgrounds.

- Simple lines can show buildings or the countryside.

- When drawing foreign locations, remember to draw what the reader imagines the location to look like.

- Drawing a bed is simple. Two ends, a piece across to bind the two and your ready to sleep.

- Just think of many items of furniture as boxes with legs.

- Keep all objects around the house simple.

- When drawing furniture, keep each piece simple. Try not to fill the drawing with objects that may hide the joke that is trying to get out.

10 DRAWING A FRIEND

It is not easy to draw the likeness of a person. In fact, it is one of the most difficult parts of cartooning and few professional cartoonists ever capture a good caricature.

So, although this is a chapter about how to draw people you know, do not feel too bad if it looks nothing like them. Most of the people that Picasso drew had two eyes on one side of the face. If he made it with drawings like that, so can you.

Where do we start? A good place is with someone you know really well.

You! All you need is a mirror, and, there in front of you, is that extremely cheap model.

Take a good look at the shape of your face.

A Is it long and narrow? This is at least a start.

B Place the eyes nose and ears in position. So far it could be anyone.

C Do you have thick eyebrows? Good. Get them down.

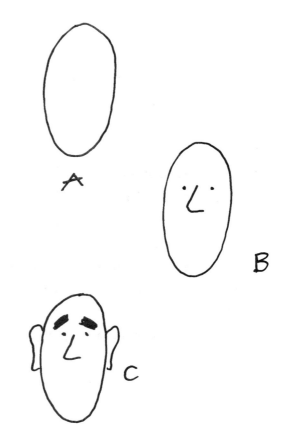

DRAWING A FRIEND

D Do you have a beard?
Better still.

E Are you wearing
glasses?
Excellent.

F Are you bald?
Wonderful.

Here is what I think
you might look like.

So it doesn't look
like you.

I tried.

We have learned that to draw
people to look the way they do is not
always easy.

Quite frankly, it is more difficult to draw you since I have never met you
or even seen a photo of you. The more we see a particular person, the
easier he or she is to draw.

Let us take an example. The people we see the most are those who
have achieved some level of fame.

Let's look at one of the most famous.

Shakespeare.

DRAWING A FRIEND

The wonderful thing about drawing this famous British playwright is the simple fact that we have plenty of pictures and paintings of what he looked like. We know that he had a moustache and a little tug of hair under the lip. Shakespeare is a perfect model.

Begin with our friendly orange shape. Now add the eyes and the nose, not much hair on top, a small moustache and some hair under the lip.

If you aim to become a political cartoonist, you will find it essential to draw politicians who are instantly recognizable. This is not as difficult as you may think. The more people appear in the media, the easier they are to draw. Who better than Bill Clinton?

Start with your orange shape and then the nose. It's quite big at the end. Add the eyes, the distinctive hair, just enlarge the shape and your drawing is finished.

DRAWING A FRIEND

Few people in the world capture the attention of the media as much as the British Royal family. Here are some examples of my drawings of this remarkable group of people.

Although Lady Diana is no longer with us, her image remains.

In this example, I decided to make a point of choosing not only a dominant feature but of also including a piece of Diana's clothing, like her hat, that could be easily associated with her.

Certainly, Prince Charles' dominant feature for a caricature is his ears.

DRAWING A FRIEND

In drawing the Queen Mother, I concentrate on her favourite hat.

Notice the features that have been caricatured in this picture.

Ears for Prince Charles and a large amount of hair for Prince Andrew. The Duke has a prominent nose, as does Lady Diana.

Each of the drawings demonstrates the importance of both features and clothes when drawing a well-known figure.

DRAWING A FRIEND

Here is the whole family, together with the Queen. See how many you can recognize.

Don't feel too discouraged if, when drawing friends, the finished cartoon does not look at all like them. To meet a famous figure in person is usually a surprise.

Accustomed as we are by the cartoons of the person, it is a surprise to find that the drawings are not nearly as accurate as we thought.

DRAWING A FRIEND

I remember meeting a politician that I had drawn over the years and found myself shocked by the colour of his hair. He was a redhead. All those years, drawing for newspapers I had always imagined that his hair was dark.

Just keep on drawing whomever you wish. Look for the outstanding features and concentrate on them.

So far we have concentrated on the face. Naturally, there's plenty more to the human than just a pretty face. Some people are large and some are thin. When I think of my favourite comedians of all time, there is the perfect mix.

Charlie Chaplin was a tiny tramp who wore a bowler hat and carried a cane. Then there was the wonderful Laurel and Hardy. One, Laurel, was thin and his close friend, Hardy, was not.

DRAWING A FRIEND

The point I'm making is this. The face is not the only feature we attempt to draw when working on a likeness. Look at the whole person and see what it is that makes that person different from everyone else.

Maybe it's size or shape, or the clothes - whatever it is that makes this person stand out from a crowd.

Here are two more drawings of famous people wearing the clothes that give them their distinct appearance. The first is the Palestinian leader, Yasha Arifat, with his familiar head scarf. The second, Uncle Sam, with his famous hat and distinctive clothes.

DRAWING A FRIEND

Keep in mind.

- Drawing a likeness is not easy.

- Begin with someone you know well, such as yourself.

- Draw yourself by looking in the mirror.

- Look for outstanding features.

- Practice by drawing famous faces.

- Try drawing the British Royal family. Look for the outstanding features for each of them.

- Use clothes to show who the person is. For example, draw the Queen Mother's hat, the Queen's glasses or Lady Di's hats.

- Study magazine photos to pick out the prominent features of various famous people.

- There's more than a face to someone's appearance. Study the whole person to find out what is different.

# 11 THE STRIP CARTOON

This is probably the most popular of all the newspaper cartoons. Most people have their favourites, whether they be For Better Or Worse, Peanuts or the newest successful kid on the block, Dilbert.

For me, the strip cartoon is the one that I try to persuade parents to encourage a cartooning child to tackle. The strip cartoon is, in effect, a play.

Whatever the number of squares, that is the number of acts.

Let's get to the most common of newspaper strip cartoons and break it up into four squares.

We have four acts to write. In the first act, we're going to introduce our performers. One is a retired, married couple who love each other very much, though, like most married couples, they argue constantly over politics.

THE STRIP CARTOON

I usually scribble four pieces of dialogue, remembering to end the play with the punch line. Once I'm satisfied that I have what I feel is a funny cartoon idea, I then set the scene by introducing our lead actors.

In the first scene of this strip cartoon, we see our actors reading the newspaper.

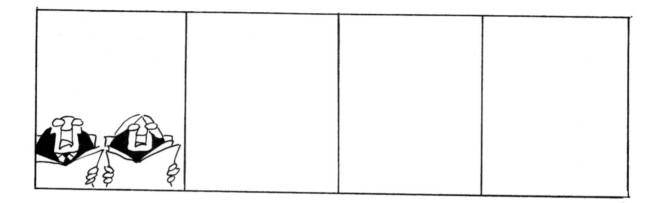

Since we know, by having written our script, that the scene is going to be the same for each of the four acts, we can now position the actors in our four-act play.

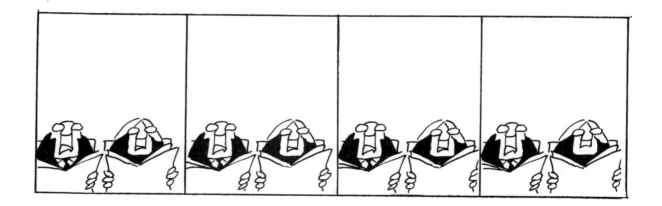

THE STRIP CARTOON

All we need now is the script. Each actor is handed this and delivers his or her lines - ending with a surprise and, hopefully, a funny finish.

I cannot emphasize enough how important it is to encourage youngsters to draw strip cartoons.

Why?

Because it's more than cartooning. They are now thinking like a playwright - writing dialogue that will hook them into writing scripts. It's no surprise that many of the world's most brilliant filmmakers began as cartoonists. The remarkable Italian director, Fellini, was an incredible cartoonist. John Huston, the great American director, was also a cartoonist. The one and only, Alfred Hitchcock, never looked through a camera. He drew hundreds of small cartoons for his film crew to follow.

Last, and by no means least, is Spielberg. He makes full use of story boards before the making of a movie. Is it any wonder that, although I appreciate that your child may want to be a cartoonist, I strongly advise you to steer them toward the strip cartoon. It's the beginning of a world of stage and film and the visual arts.

THE STRIP CARTOON

Before we finish this chapter, let us have one more look at drawing your own strip cartoon. Most successful strip cartoonists draw cartoons that deal with a subject they know well.

Peanuts, a cartoon that features the adventures of a group of children, was drawn by Charles Schultz, a man who had children of his own. On the other hand, the British cartoon, Andy Capp, featured a British character who seemed to spend most of his time at football matches and in the pub. No children ever appeared. Why? Because the artist, a happily married Reg Smythe, had no children. The wonderful Canadian cartoonist, Lynne Johnson, is married to a dentist, has children of her own and a family dog. Who appears in the strip 'For Better Or Worse"? Lynne's real live family.

So choose a subject you know well and begin to draw.

Since I am a senior, I have some idea of how they think. Let's continue with a Bill and Mavis strip.

I begin by scribbling out on a piece of paper various ideas. I have decided that Bill and Mavis are walking through the park discussing politics.

Did you ever consider going into Politics, Bill?

Many times, but I was never sure I could get enough votes, Mavis

Don't you mean vote?

No, Mavis— I mean votes!

THE STRIP CARTOON

Now that I am happy with the idea, I once again draw the squares for
my four act play. I make sure that the line dividing each of the squares
is in the middle of the strip. This allows editors to place them on top
of each other rather than straight across the newspaper - the usual
straight across method.

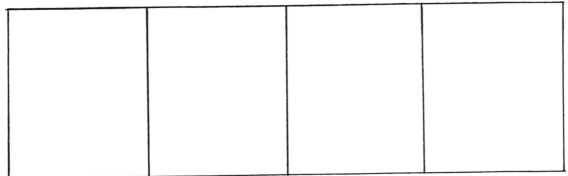

MIDDLE
LINE

The split version is with two panels on top of
each other.

We are ready to draw our strip. Continue to
think of the strip as a short film and use film
terminology. In the first scene, we have a close
up. The second scene is a close up of Bill. The
third scene is a long shot of Bill and Mavis in the
park. The last scene is a close up of both Mavis
and Bill showing their facial reactions.

THE STRIP CARTOON

Another reminder.

- Think of the strip as a play.

- The number of squares equals the number of acts - four squares equals four acts.

- Introduce performers.

- Position the actors in the squares.

- Write your script so that it ends with a punch line.

- Many famous film directors started as cartoonists.

- Draw what you know. How about a strip revolving around your life?

- Make sure the strip you draw can be easily split down the middle to make a strip of two panels on top and two on the bottom.

- Think of your cartoon strip as a movie. Use various angles, such as close ups, long shots and tight 'camera' angles.

CLOSE UP

LONG SHOT

TIGHT SHOT

12 THINKING OF A JOKE

The first thing to understand is that humour is extremely personal. What one person may find funny, others will find bores the pants off them. The secret is to find more of your readers who think the jokes are funny than readers who don't.

Political cartoons that depict someone we know are particularly funny. Especially if the person in the cartoon is someone who holds an important position. Certainly, most politicians find it difficult to overcome their reputation of bending the truth. For this reason, the subject is a favourite of the political cartoonists.

THINKING OF A JOKE

Many cartoons present the characters in a particularly sad situation. Why? Because humour and tragedy run side by side. Probably the most commonly used by cartoonists is the desert island joke. There are millions of them. Here is one idea. Why not try a few of your own?

There are many other drawings that can give you a kick start when you try to think up ideas. Here are some of the most popular.

A heaven joke.   A telephone joke.

THINKING OF A JOKE

Or how about a fortune teller joke?

Or a William Tell joke?

THINKING OF A JOKE

These single drawing jokes are known in the business as 'one panel' cartoons. The beauty of them is that they take very little time to draw. Many people ask me the question, "What comes first, the drawing or the idea?" This depends on whether I have an idea in my head that I wish to get down on paper or have just arrived in the office and have grabbed some paper. I then begin to scribble various figures and then add the conversation.

Let's try this. Scribble a group who have met on the street. Two of them are women friends who have obviously been shopping. Standing beside the one who is talking is a man.

Now sit back and begin to write various lines of dialogue that the woman could be saying to her friend. Here's the idea I had.

"I was waiting for the right man to come along and finally said, 'To hell with it'."

THINKING OF A JOKE

Important reminder.

- What one person thinks is funny another may find boring.

- A good joke can often be turned into a good cartoon.

- Humour and tragedy run side by side.

- Try the most common joke, the desert island.

- Try other joke situations.

- Single panel jokes are known as one panel cartoons.

- Scribble a group on the street and write a line underneath.

13 DRAWING ANIMALS

We are all part of the animal kingdom, so the rules that we have followed for drawing the human are no different.

Let's draw as we did earlier - a stick figure of an animal that is the favourite of most people. This is the elephant.

Grab your pencil and make a rough start by getting the figure down in it's simplest form.

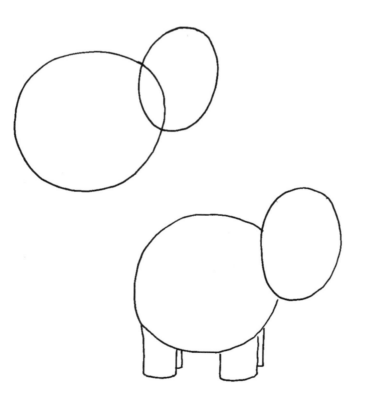

Begin with a rough oval for the body. Now draw the head.

Add the legs, remove the lines between the head and body and we're on our way.

DRAWING ANIMALS

Now add the ears and trunk.

Finish off with the tail, the eyes and a few details like toe nails.

Since this was so easy, let's try a few more animals. There are certainly enough of them to go around. The problem for most of us is remembering what many of the animals look like.

Don't be afraid to go to a reference book. Many cartoonists do this when looking for a specific animal or bird. Better yet, if you feel that the animal is the kind of cartoon you enjoy drawing, get a good illustrated book of animals.

DRAWING ANIMALS

Take the same steps that you did when drawing the elephant and, before you know it, you'll have a complete zoo.

One other point to remember. We are cartoonists and, as such, are not producing a serious drawing of an animal. It's a cartoon. To give you an idea of what I mean, let's try drawing one of the funnier looking animals around - the giraffe.

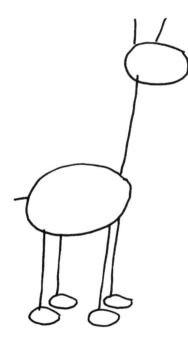

Again, start with a rough outline using our stick figure as our starting point.

Add the details and you have a giraffe that Noah would have been proud to welcome on board his ark.

DRAWING ANIMALS

As we race through our imaginary jungle, we'll find that not all animals have legs. How many can you think of?

Here's an obvious.

Even this creature we can begin by drawing as a stick figure.

Maybe you live on a farm. Then you will certainly find lots of animals to draw.

Just for fun, here are a few that you may have seen around the yard.

DRAWING ANIMALS

Fortunately, there are animals with whom we are all familiar. They are the ones that we count as part of the family. For this reason, many cartoonists include them in their cartoons. I'm speaking of the cat and the dog.

If you have one or both, take a look at them. Now make a nice, quick stick figure drawing and see where it takes us. We can begin with a favourite of many cartoonists - the cat.

Once again, it's back to the old stick figure, with the circles for a head and sticks for legs. Good.

Now try drawing a cat of your own. Here are a few of mine.

DRAWING ANIMALS

One thing we should be aware of is that all cartoonists draw their animals the way they see them.

Take a good look in your local newspaper and you'll certainly see some wonderful examples of animals that spend their time dashing through the comic strips.

For sure, each and every one of them will be funny to look at.

Keep this in mind as you draw a cartoon dog.

DRAWING ANIMALS

Once again we can begin with the stick figure.

Maybe the only pet you have in the house is a fish.

DRAWING ANIMALS

No cartoon book would be complete without drawings of birds. They are, of course, the easiest of subjects to tackle, provided they are flying.

Bird flying.   A close up of a bird flying.

Just joking. To get serious, once more with the stick figure. We'll need our round shapes for heads, and sticks for wings and legs.

Although we have come to the end of our book, for you, it's just the beginning. You are now a cartoonist.

So grab that paper and pen, and get drawing. See? Didn't I tell you it was fun!

DRAWING ANIMALS

One last reminder...

- Drawing animals and humans are no different.

- Start with the stick figure.

- Try drawing an elephant.

- Don't be afraid to look at illustrations of animals.

- You're drawing a cartoon animal. It's supposed to look funny.

- Not all animals have legs.

- Try drawing farm animals.

- Now draw the pets around the house.

- **HAVE FUN!**